PENNSYLVANIA

by Dana Meachen Rau
and Jonatha A. Brown

GARETH**STEVENS**
PUBLISHING
A Member of the WRC Media Family of Companies

Please visit our web site at: www.garethstevens.com
For a free color catalog describing Gareth Stevens Publishing's
list of high-quality books and multimedia programs, call
1-800-542-2595 (USA) or 1-800-387-3178 (Canada).
Gareth Stevens Publishing's fax: (877) 542-2596.

Library of Congress Cataloging-in-Publication Data

Rau, Dana Meachen, 1971-
    Pennsylvania / Dana Meachen Rau and Jonatha A. Brown.
      p. cm. — (Portraits of the states)
    Includes bibliographical references and index.
    ISBN-10: 0-8368-4633-8   ISBN-13: 978-0-8368-4633-1 (lib. bdg.)
    ISBN-10: 0-8368-4652-4   ISBN-13: 978-0-8368-4652-2 (softcover)
    1. Pennsylvania—Juvenile literature.   I. Brown, Jonatha A.
    II. Title. III. Series.
    F149.3.R38   2005
    974.8—dc22   2005042672

Updated edition reprinted in 2007. First published in 2006 by
Gareth Stevens Publishing
A Weekly Reader Company
1 Reader's Digest Rd.
Pleasantville, NY 10570-7000 USA

Copyright © 2006 by Gareth Stevens, Inc.

Editorial direction: Mark J. Sachner
Project manager: Jonatha A. Brown
Editor: Betsy Rasmussen
Art direction and design: Tammy West
Picture research: Diane Laska-Swanke
Indexer: Walter Kronenberg
Production: Jessica Morris and Robert Kraus

Picture credits: Cover, p. 25 © CORBIS; pp. 4, 5, 9 © Corel; p. 6 © North Wind
Picture Archives; p. 11 © MPI/Getty Images; p. 15 © PhotoDisc; pp. 16, 21, 22,
24, 26 © Gibson Stock Photography; p. 27 © Tom Hauck/Getty Images; p. 29
© Hulton Archive/Getty Images

Printed in the United States of America

1 2 3 4 5 6 7 8 9 09 08 07

CONTENTS

Words that are defined in the Glossary appear
in **bold** the first time they are used in the text.

On the Cover: The Pittsburgh skyline combines elements of the city's
historic past and dynamic present.

Introduction

Welcome to Pennsylvania! Here, you can ski in the mountains. You can go boating on rivers and lakes. You can see famous works of art and go to folk festivals.

This lovely state is full of history, too. You can visit old battlefields. You can see where American leaders once wrote the rules for a new government.

Winter and summer, indoors and out, there is always something interesting to do. So, come for a visit. Come to explore! The people of Pennsylvania are eager to show you their state.

These cannons stand at Valley Forge. George Washington and his soldiers spent a long, cold winter in Valley Forge during the American Revolution.

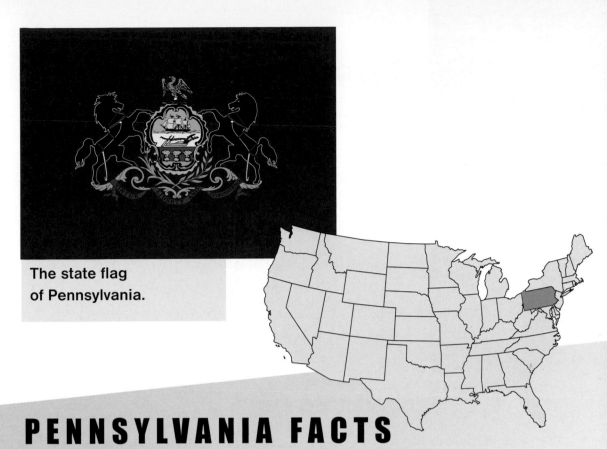

The state flag
of Pennsylvania.

PENNSYLVANIA FACTS

- Became the 2nd State: December 12, 1787
- Population (2006): 12,440,621
- Capital: Harrisburg
- Biggest Cities: Philadelphia, Pittsburgh, Allentown, Erie
- Size: 44,817 square miles (116,076 square kilometers)
- Nickname: The Keystone State
- State Tree: Hemlock
- State Flower: Mountain laurel
- State Animal: White-tailed deer
- State Bird: Ruffed grouse

History

Native Americans were the first people to live in Pennsylvania. They came to the area more than ten thousand years ago. Many Native groups lived in the river valleys. Some fought with each other.

In 1608, the British explored the area. Captain John Smith led the way. The first settlers came from Sweden and lived on Tinicum Island. Later, the Dutch claimed the region. Finally, Britain took over in 1664. Britain held many **colonies** along the East Coast.

British Colony

William Penn was a Quaker. In Britain, he and others of the Quaker faith did not feel welcome. In 1681, the British king gave some land in America to William Penn. Penn founded the colony of Pennsylvania. People who lived

William Penn met with Native people. They agreed to share the land.

Settlers and Native Americans

When white people came to Pennsylvania, life changed for the Natives. The settlers brought diseases with them, and many Natives got sick and died. Some Natives fought the settlers. In 1763, the fighting ended, and the settlers won. Most of the Natives were forced to move west.

there could practice their own religions. They could live the way they wanted. They could own land.

Penn also founded the city of Philadelphia. Many people from Britain came to live there. The town grew quickly. Before long, it was the most important city in the colonies.

Not all of the early settlers were British. Many were German, Scottish, and Irish.

Some of these early settlers owned African slaves. By the mid-1700s, about four thousand slaves lived in the area.

A Battleground

Both France and Britain wanted the land in America. In 1754, they began fighting for it. They fought the French and Indian War. Many Natives fought in this war, too. Some fought on one side, and some fought on the other. Many battles

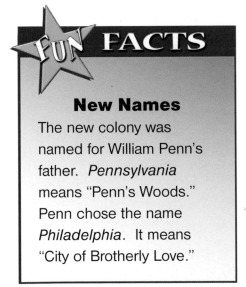

FUN FACTS

New Names
The new colony was named for William Penn's father. *Pennsylvania* means "Penn's Woods." Penn chose the name *Philadelphia*. It means "City of Brotherly Love."

FUN FACTS

The Importance of Philadelphia

Philadelphia played a big part in U.S. history in the early days. Colonial leaders met there to plan the war against Britain. They wrote the Declaration of Independence there, too. Later, they came back to write the U.S. Constitution. This great city was also the U.S. capital for ten years.

battles took place in Pennsylvania. The British took over Philadelphia for almost one year. The war finally ended in 1783. The colonists won. The new and

Famous People of Pennsylvania

Andrew Carnegie

Born: November 25, 1835, Dunfermline, Fife, Scotland

Died: August 11, 1919, Lenox, Massachusetts

Andrew Carnegie moved to Pittsburgh when he was a boy. He worked for a railroad company and made a great deal of money. After the Civil War, he started a company that made iron railroad bridges. Later, he started a steel business. He soon owned coal and iron mines and steel mills. He became one of the richest men in the world! Carnegie used some of his money to help build libraries all over the country.

of this war took place in Pennsylvania.

The British won the war after nine years of fighting. Now, Britain held thirteen colonies along the East Coast. Many colonists soon grew tired of British rule. They wanted to be free. In 1775, they began fighting for their freedom in the Revolutionary War. Many

independent country was called the United States of America.

Mining State

Pennsylvania became a U.S. state in 1787. The state grew rich. Its mines provided iron for tools and building materials. Coal was mined, too. Coal produced a fire hot enough to melt, or **smelt**, iron ore.

The Declaration of Independence was signed in Philadelphia in 1776.

Later, oil was discovered in Pennsylvania. The state became the top oil producer in the country.

The first railroads were built in the 1800s. **Canals** were dug at this time, too. Now trains and ships could carry iron, coal, and oil to markets far away.

In 1781, Pennsylvania became the first state to ban slavery. Many people in northern states were against slavery. Most white people

The Underground Railroad

In the South, many slaves ran away from their owners in the first half of the 1800s. Two men from Pennsylvania, Robert Porter and William Still, helped slaves escape. They set up the Underground Railroad. This was not a train on tracks. It was a group of people who hid runaway slaves. They helped slaves to escape without being caught. Thanks to the Underground Railroad, many slaves reached the safety of the North.

country called the Confederate States of America. Northern states did not want the country to split. From 1861 to 1865, the two sides fought the Civil War. Pennsylvania fought on the side of the North. The war ended in 1865. The North won. The South rejoined the United States. Slavery was now against the law in all states.

Steel State

After the war, Pennsylvania became an industrial giant. Its rich reserves of iron were used to make steel. Soon, the state was a center for steel production.

At that time, people from Europe arrived by the thousands. Some worked in iron and coal mines. Others worked in iron and steel **mills**. These mills were

in southern states approved of slavery. Many people in southern states used slaves to work on their farms.

Southern states finally broke away from the North. They formed their own

The Battle of Gettysburg
During the Civil War, Gettysburg was the scene of an awful battle. More than fifty thousand soldiers died or were hurt. Later, President Abraham Lincoln gave a famous speech in Gettysburg. He honored the soldiers who had fought there. He urged people to keep fighting for freedom and fairness.

huge **factories** that shaped the metals into building materials and tools. Pittsburgh, Bethlehem, and other steel cities grew and thrived.

Steel from Pennsylvania helped the whole country grow, too. It was used to build railroads. It was also used in skyscrapers. These tall buildings became common in some cities.

The mines and mills made many people rich in the late 1800s. Yet workers in these places were often poor. Most worked for low pay. Some

The bloodiest battle of the Civil War was fought at Gettysburg.

11

worked in places that were dangerous. If a worker was hurt on the job, he or she could not earn money to raise a family. Many workers began to join **unions**. They said they would not work until the problems were solved. Unions became very powerful. They helped workers get higher pay and safer places to work.

The Twentieth Century and Beyond

In the 1900s, the United States fought in two big wars — World War I and World War II. Factories in Pennsylvania made guns, ships, planes, and tanks to fight these wars. After World War II, the state struggled. The demand for coal dropped off. Some businesses moved to other states. In Pennsylvania, mines and mills closed.

On September 11, 2001, a terrible event made the news. Terrorists took over four planes. As one flew over western Pennsylvania, it crashed in a field. Many people died. People all over the world were shocked.

Today, the people of Pennsylvania are bringing new types of jobs to the state.

IN PENNSYLVANIA'S HISTORY

Nuclear Power

In the 1950s, Pennsylvania led the way in the nuclear age. It was home to the first **nuclear power plant** in the world. This plant was in Shippingport. In 1979, another nuclear power plant in the state made the news. The plant on Three Mile Island had a leak. The leak was dangerous and frightening, but no one was hurt. It was the first big nuclear accident in the country. Since then, many changes have been made. Now, nuclear power is safer.

★ ★ ★ Time Line ★ ★ ★

1608	Captain John Smith first explores the area.
1664	The British take control of the area.
1776	The Declaration of Independence is written and signed in Philadelphia.
1781	Pennsylvania outlaws slavery.
1787	The Constitution is written and signed in Philadelphia. Pennsylvania becomes the second U.S. state.
1790–1800	Philadelphia is the capital of the United States.
1857–1861	James Buchanan of Pennsylvania serves as U.S. president.
1863	Soldiers fight in the Battle of Gettysburg during the Civil War.
1873	Andrew Carnegie opens large steel companies.
1889	Many people die when a flood destroys Johnstown.
1979	Three Mile Island power plant has the worst nuclear accident in U.S. history.
2001	Terrorists take over a plane that crashes in Pennsylvania.

People

More than twelve million people live in Pennsylvania. Most live in or near cities. About one person in four lives around the two biggest cities. They are Philadelphia and Pittsburgh. Many people also make their homes in **rural** areas. More people in Pennsylvania live in rural areas than any other U.S. state.

Pennsylvania has a mix of people. In the early days, Natives lived on the land. Then, most early settlers came from

Hispanics: In the 2000 U.S. Census, 3.2 percent of the people in Pennsylvania called themselves Latino or Hispanic. Most of them or their relatives came from places where Spanish is spoken. They may come from different racial backgrounds.

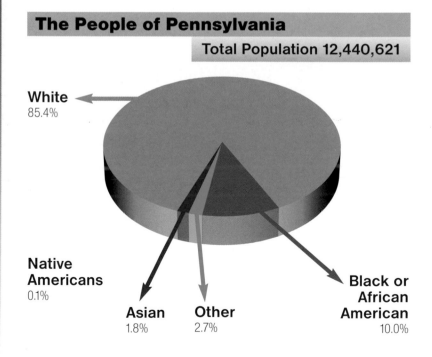

The People of Pennsylvania

Total Population 12,440,621

White
85.4%

Native Americans
0.1%

Asian
1.8%

Other
2.7%

Black or African American
10.0%

Percentages are based on 2000 Census.

The city of Philadelphia rises along the banks of the Delaware River.

Europe. Later, runaway slaves came from southern states. People are still coming to the state from far away. These days, many people come from Mexico, China, and India. Native Americans are one of the smallest groups living in Pennsylvania. Now, only about eleven thousand Natives live in Pennsylvania.

The Pennsylvania Dutch

The state is known for a group of people called the Pennsylvania Dutch. They first arrived about three hundred years ago. They wanted to be free to practice their religion. Most of these people became farmers in southern parts of the state.

More than seventy-five thousand Pennsylvania Dutch still live in the state. Some of these people are

The Amish use horses instead of tractors on their farms. They do not drive cars or have electricity in their homes.

Amish. The Amish wear plain clothing. Most do not have electricity or telephones in their homes. They do not use tractors to farm their land. Instead, they use plows pulled by horses or oxen. They use horses and buggies to travel, just as people did before cars were invented.

Religion and Education

Most people in the state are Christians. The Pennsylvania Dutch are Christians. Other Christians in the state include Catholics and Baptists. Quakers founded Pennsylvania, but very few Quakers still live there. In fact, more Jews and Muslims live in Pennsylvania than Quakers.

The people of Pennsylvania have always

cared about learning. When the colony was young, the law said all children should know how to read and write.

In 1689, early Quakers started the Friends' Public School in Philadelphia. This school is still running. It is now called the William Penn Charter School.

In 1834, the state created public schools. Pennsylvania was the second state in the country to have public schools.

Benjamin Franklin founded the University of Pennsylvania in Philadelphia. It was the first U.S. college to accept people of all religious faiths. Today, people come from all over the world to go to school there.

Famous People of Pennsylvania

Benjamin Franklin

Born: January 17, 1706, Boston, Massachusetts

Died: April 17, 1790, Philadelphia, Pennsylvania

Benjamin Franklin lived in Philadelphia for many years. He was well known as a printer, a writer, and an **inventor**. He also started the first library in the colonies. Later, he became a great leader. He signed the Declaration of Independence. He also helped write the U.S. Constitution. As an old man, he was one of the most famous Americans in the world. Now, Franklin is known as one of the country's **Founding Fathers**.

The Land

Pennsylvania is crisscrossed by rivers and mountains. The mountains once made travel very hard. In those days, the rivers were a good way to get from place to place. By following rivers, people could get past mountains without having to climb them.

Waterways

The northwest corner of the state borders Lake Erie. Lake Erie is one of the five Great Lakes. It provides a water route to the Atlantic Ocean. There are no big lakes within Pennsylvania. The largest lake is man-made, and it measures only 26 square miles (67 square km). It is the Pymatuning Reservoir.

The longest river in Pennsylvania is the Ohio River. It is in the western part of the state. The Delaware River is on the other side of the state. It runs along the eastern border. Philadelphia was built on the banks of the Delaware River.

In the past, the rivers of Pennsylvania have caused great damage. The city of Johnstown has flooded three times. It is on the Conemaugh River.

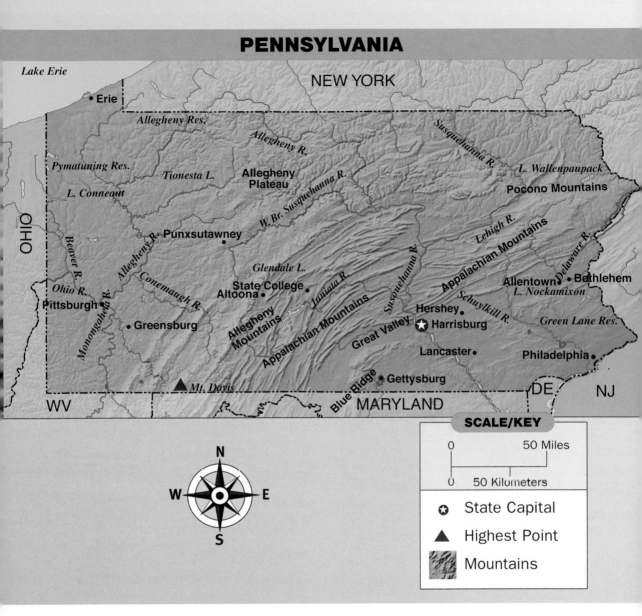

PENNSYLVANIA

Lake Erie

NEW YORK

• Erie

Allegheny Res.

Allegheny R.

Susquehanna R.

Pymatuning Res.

Tionesta L.

Allegheny
Plateau

L. Wallenpaupack

L. Conneaut

W. Br. Susquehanna R.

Pocono Mountains

OHIO

Beaver R.

Allegheny R. • Punxsutawney

Lehigh R.

Appalachian Mountains

Delaware R.

Glendale L.

Conemaugh R.

State College •
Altoona •

Juniata R.

Susquehanna R.

Allentown • • Bethlehem
L. Nockamixon

Ohio R.
Pittsburgh •

Allegheny
Mountains

Schuylkill R.

Hershey •
⭐ Harrisburg

Green Lane Res.

Monongahela R.

• Greensburg

Appalachian Mountains

Great Valley

Lancaster •

Philadelphia •

▲ *Mt. Davis*

Blue Ridge • Gettysburg

DE

NJ

WV

MARYLAND

SCALE/KEY

0	50 Miles
0	50 Kilometers

⭐ State Capital

▲ Highest Point

Mountains

N
W E
S

In 1889, heavy rains fell. A dam on the river broke, and a flood killed more than two thousand people. This area also flooded in 1936 and 1977. Many lives were lost.

The Lay of the Land

Much of the land in this state is mountainous or hilly. In the north and west stand many ridges and valleys.

The Allegheny Mountains run along the lower edge of this area. Mt. Davis, the highest peak in the state, stands in these mountains. It is 3,213 feet (979 meters) high. The state has two more mountain ranges. One is the Appalachian Mountains. They stand further east. The Pocono

Major Rivers

Ohio River
975 miles (1,569 km) long

Susquehanna River
444 miles (714 km) long

Allegheny River
325 miles (523 km) long

Mountains are in the northeast.

Only two parts of the state are fairly flat. The land in the northwest corner, near Lake Erie, is quite flat. The soil is sandy there, so fruits and vegetables grow well. **Plains** and low hills cover southeastern Pennsylvania. The soil is rich, and much of the land is farmed. As the plains approach the Delaware River, this land becomes very flat and low.

Plants and Animals

More than half of Pennsylvania is covered by

FUN FACTS

Deep Down

Millions of years ago, big movements of the earth caused mountains to form in Pennsylvania. Some of these mountains were formed over ancient swamps. Much later, thick sheets of ice swept across the land. The mountains pressed down on the swamps below. This pressure turned the swamplands into huge beds of coal.

forests. Maple, oak, pine, and many other types of trees grow there. Mountain laurel, the state flower, colors the countryside.

The forests offer homes to many animals. Black bears are found in the north and west. Deer, raccoons, and squirrels live all over the state. Pheasants and wild turkeys are common, and fish swim the rivers and lakes.

FUN FACTS

Groundhog Day

February 2 is Groundhog Day! Once a year, on this day, people gather in Punxsutawney, Pennsylvania. They wait for the groundhog Punxsutawney Phil to come out of his burrow. **Custom** says that if he sees his shadow, there will be six more weeks of winter. If not, then spring will soon arrive.

Climate

The weather in Pennsylvania changes with the seasons. In summer, it is warm. In some parts of the state, it can also be very humid. In winter, it is cold. The northern and western parts of the state are the coldest and get the most snow.

The Monongahela River runs through the southwestern part of the state.

Economy

Pennsylvania has been changing with the times. Iron and coal are still mined. Steel is still produced. Yet they are not as important as they once were. These days, electrical equipment and chemicals are the top products of the state.

Fewer people work in factories now. More people work in stores or in service jobs. Service workers help other people. They work in hospitals, hotels, schools, and places people visit.

Railroads helped the state grow. Trains carried coal, iron, and steel to markets all over the country.

Farms still cover about one-third of the land. Milk is the leading farm product. Eggs and beef cattle are important, too. Pennsylvania also grows more mushrooms than any other state. Large amounts of hay, corn, apples, and other fruits are harvested every year.

Transportation

Back in 1794, the first paved road ran from Philadelphia to Lancaster. By the 1860s, the state had more paved roads than any other state. It had more miles of railroad, too. Railroads gave a big boost to the steel business.

Pennsylvania has long been a center for shipping. Philadelphia is the largest freshwater **port** in the world. Pittsburgh and Erie are also big ports. The state's roads, railroads, rivers, and ports are all good for business.

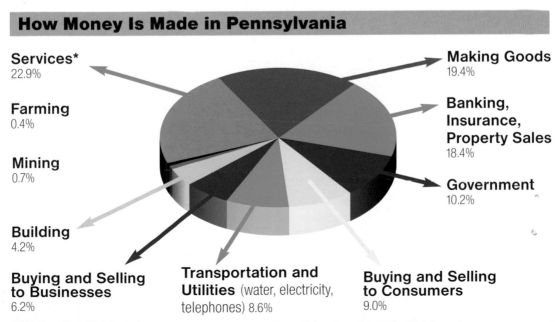

How Money Is Made in Pennsylvania

Services*
22.9%

Farming
0.4%

Mining
0.7%

Building
4.2%

Buying and Selling to Businesses
6.2%

Transportation and Utilities (water, electricity, telephones) 8.6%

Buying and Selling to Consumers
9.0%

Making Goods
19.4%

Banking, Insurance, Property Sales
18.4%

Government
10.2%

* Services include jobs in hotels, restaurants, auto repair, medicine, teaching, and entertainment.

Government

Harrisburg is the capital of Pennsylvania. The state's leaders work there. The government has three parts, or branches. They are the executive, legislative, and judicial branches.

Executive Branch

A governor leads the executive branch. Many other people work for the governor. Their job is to carry out the laws of the state.

Legislative Branch

The legislature is called the General Assembly. It has two parts. They are called the Senate and the House of

Harrisburg has been the capital of Pennsylvania since 1812. The state capitol building can be recognized by its domed roof.

Independence Hall stands in Philadelphia. Both the Declaration of Independence and the U.S. Constitution were written and signed in this great hall.

Representatives. They work together to make new state laws.

Judicial Branch

Judges and courts make up the judicial branch. Judges and courts may decide whether people who have been **accused of** committing crimes are guilty.

Local Governments

The state is made up of sixty-seven counties. Within the counties are townships cities, and boroughs. Each has its own government. In some cases, city and county governments are combined.

PENNSYLVANIA'S STATE GOVERNMENT

Executive		Legislative		Judicial	
Office	**Length of Term**	**Body**	**Length of Term**	**Court**	**Length of Term**
Governor	4 years	Senate (50 members)	4 years	Supreme (7 justices)	10 years
Lieutenant Governor	4 years	House of Representatives (203 members)	2 years	Intermediate appellate courts (24 justices)	10 years

Things to See and Do

Pennsylvania is a great place to live or visit! It has museums, historic parks, and fine sports teams.

The Liberty Bell is on display in Philadelphia. Millions of tourists come to see the bell each year.

In Philadelphia, **tourists** stroll through parks. They look at the Liberty Bell and visit Independence Hall. Early leaders met in this great hall to talk about the country and its future.

The Franklin Institute is fun, too. It is one of the best science museums in the nation. Art lovers head to the famous Philadelphia Museum of Art. The city also has a well-known orchestra. To hear one of its concerts is a treat.

Pittsburgh is also a fun city to visit. The Carnegie Institute is known for its library, art museums, and science museums.

Pennsylvania's Pro Sports Teams

Pennsylvania's two biggest cities, Philadelphia and Pittsburgh, are home to all of the state's big-league sports teams.

- Football:
  Pittsburgh Steelers
  Philadelphia Eagles
- Baseball:
  Philadelphia Phillies
  Pittsburgh Pirates
- Basketball:
  Philadelphia 76ers
- Hockey:
  Philadelphia Flyers
  Pittsburgh Penguins

The Pittsburgh Symphony Orchestra plays in Heinz Hall. These places draw visitors from around the state and the country.

More to See and Do

Valley Forge draws many visitors, too. Soldiers camped there in the 1770s. At Gettysburg, people see where a bloody battle was fought. In Hershey, visitors tour a chocolate museum.

The Pittsburgh Steelers met the New York Jets in the 2005 AFC playoffs. The Steelers won this game with a final score of 20-17.

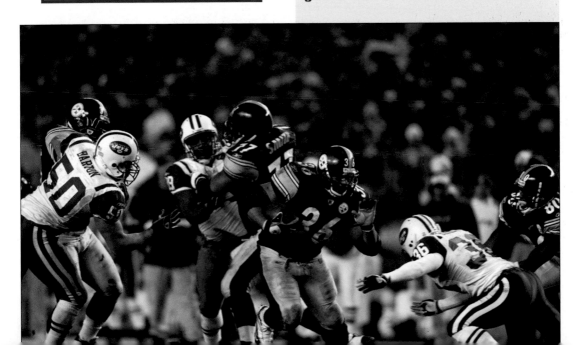

Famous People of Pennsylvania

Bill Cosby

Born: July 12, 1937, Philadelphia, Pennsylvania

As a boy, William Henry Cosby Jr. knew how to make people laugh. He could act, too. In the 1960s, he became the first black actor to co-star in a TV **drama** series. He won awards for his work on the show. Years later, he returned to TV. His hit show, "The Cosby Show," was about an African American family. He has also created cartoon characters and written books. Both children and adults enjoy Cosby's work.

These places offer a peek at Pennsylvania's past.

Many people like to visit Lancaster County. Thousands of Pennsylvania Dutch still live there. Some of them sell folk art and homemade foods. Visitors to Lancaster County like to buy these items to take home.

In the fall, football fans head to a city named State College. They try to get tickets for a Nittany Lions game. The Lions are one of the best college teams in sports history. They play for Pennsylvania State University. Fans pack the stadium for their games.

FUN FACTS

The Pennsylvania Dutch

Most people think that the Pennsylvania Dutch came from the Netherlands, or Holland. They actually came from Germany. In the German language, *Deutsch* means "German." Over the years, *Deutsch* became "Dutch," and the name stuck!

Louisa May Alcott wrote *Little Women* based on her own family.

Famous People of Pennsylvania

Louisa May Alcott

Born: November 29, 1832, Germantown, Pennsylvania

Died: March 6, 1888, Boston, Massachusetts

Louisa May Alcott grew up in a poor family. She worked as a servant and a teacher to earn money. Alcott became a famous writer. Her most famous book is *Little Women*. It was published in 1868. The book tells the story of four sisters. It was based on her own family and childhood. People all over the country still read and enjoy her books.

Special Events

Many cities and towns hold festivals and fairs. Musikfest takes place in Bethlehem. It lasts for ten days and includes more than one thousand free performances. Kutztown hosts a German festival. It features German music and the arts and crafts of the Pennsylvania Dutch.

Greensburg hosts the Westmoreland Fair. It has been going on for more than fifty years. People come to enjoy food, rides, crafts, and the prize animals on display.

accused of — blamed for

canals — man-made rivers

colonies — groups of people living in a new land but ruled, or governed, by the place they came from

custom — a way of doing things that has been followed for a long time

drama — a TV program that is intended to be serious rather than funny

factories — buildings where goods and products are made

Founding Fathers — the men who led the country in its early days

inventor — someone who creates something new

mills — buildings and machines in which something is made to sell

nuclear power plant — a place where energy is produced

plains — flat or gently rolling land that has few trees

port — a city harbor where boats can load and unload goods

rural — coming from or existing in the country

smelt — to melt metal

tourists — people who travel for pleasure

unions — a group that tries to make pay and working conditions better for workers in a factory or other business

Books

An Amish Year. Richard Ammon (Atheneum)

The Gettysburg Address. Abraham Lincoln (Houghton Mifflin)

K Is for Keystone: A Pennsylvania Alphabet. Discover America State by State (series). Kristen Kane (Thomson Gale)

Pennsylvania. From Sea to Shining Sea (series). Barbara A. Somervill (Children's Press)

Pennsylvania Facts and Symbols. The States and Their Symbols (series). Emily McAuliffe (Bridgestone Books)

The Story of William Penn. Aliki (Simon and Schuster Children's Publishing)

Valley Forge. Richard Ammon (Holiday House)

Web Sites

Historic Valley Forge
www.ushistory.org/valleyforge/

Independence Hall National Historic Park
www.nps.gov/inde/

The Pennsylvania Dutch Country Welcome Center
www.800padutch.com